INSTEAD OF DEATH

BY WILLIAM STRINGFELLOW

THE SEABURY PRESS • NEW YORK

Prepared under the auspices of the Department of Christian Education, Protestant Episcopal Church.

Some of the material here appeared in other forms in the *Christian Century*, the *Witness*, and the *International Journal of Religious Education* or was introduced in addresses at the University of South Carolina, Princeton Theological Seminary, the 1960 Strasbourg Conference of the World's Student Christian Federation, and the American Lutheran Church Student Conference of 1963.

Biblical quotations are from the Revised Standard Version.

441-863-Hm-10

for
WAYNE FIELDS

Contents

Otherwise, what do people mean by being baptized on behalf of the dead? If the dead are not raised at all, why are people baptized on their behalf?

I Corinthians 15:29

1

The Presence and Power of Death

> *For as by a man came death, by a man has come*
> *also the resurrection of the dead. For as in Adam*
> *all die, so also in Christ shall all be made alive.*
>
> I Corinthians 15:21–22

THIS IS a book about death.

It consists of some essays about the specific reality of death in contemporary life: about the vitality of the presence and power of death over human existence and, indeed, over the whole of creation. The suggestion here is that the power of death can be identified in American society—as well as elsewhere for that matter—as that which appears to be the decisive, reigning, ultimate power. Therefore, for an individual's own little life—yours or mine or anybody's —death is the reality that has the most immediate, personal, everyday significance. In this life, it seems as if everyone and everything finds meaning, when we really come down to it, in death.

No ambition is expressed here to treat the presence and activity of death exhaustively, but only to deal with it suggestively, that is, to say enough to provoke some further thought and consideration of the matter, to suggest only enough to convince the reader that it is not possible to be a human being very long without coming to terms in one way or another with the presence of death in one's own life and in the relationships between one's own life and the lives of all others and all things.

Signs of Death in Urban Life

The particular focus here is upon the signs of death and evidences of the activity of death in American urban culture, especially as they impinge upon a person in daily life and work. That focus is chosen, for one thing, because the city is my own habitat; it is the place I know. But also the city represents some sort of fruition of American society or, perhaps more precisely, the city represents some sort of terminal point of American society. Be that as it may, the city increasingly dominates the whole of American life—just as, earlier, colonialism or, later on, the frontier did—and no one escapes involvement—politically, economically, culturally, psychologically, personally—with the city, whether he recognizes it or likes it or not.

The city is the place today where all the forces, purposes, powers, and factors dispersed throughout society generally have been congregated and brought into radical, complex, and delicate juxtaposition with one another. You do not escape the issues of modern American urban life by living in Bangor or San Jose, or on a farm in Iowa, and you certainly do not mitigate them by moving out of New York to Darien or Scarsdale. You cannot even hide from the same issues in Magnolia, Mississippi. The issues of urban life permeate the whole society and culture of the United States, and the question is not whether they can be avoided or whether you can somehow hide from them, but how you or I or anyone else come to terms with them and whether we will confront them with intelligence and frankness.

Moreover, you need not live in Manhattan or Detroit rather than Evanston or Amherst to recognize the common problems of human life. In the slums and in the suburbs, among both poor and rich, for black as well as white, to older people as much as the young, for both sexes, among the uneducated and the more learned, the lives of people encompass buying and selling, fighting and forgiving, work and play, illness and health, hate and love, living for awhile in all these ways and then dying and, after a time, being forgotten. The significant issues of life are everywhere essentially the same for every person as they are for you or me.

Although these issues are as much present and serious outside the city as within the city, they are more obvious and open in the city, perhaps more exaggerated in the city, maybe more dramatized there. Certainly in the city they are evident in a magnitude and scope and concentration that makes it impossible to ignore them or to pretend that they are not there. And, hence, by looking at the city, one glimpses the whole American scene so far as the ordinary human issues are concerned.

Remembering that this book is to be suggestive, not exhaustive, provocative, not definitive, attention is concentrated only on certain issues that mark the life of a person, particularly a young person, in today's urban culture. These issues—seen here as signs of the power of death at work in American society—are loneliness, sex and the search for personal identity, work, leisure, and security.

Such issues cannot, of course, be neatly isolated one from another, or from a host of other issues which might also be raised. The underlying thought in this book is that they are most profoundly related by that to which each of them is a witness in the common experience of people: *death*. Death, in other words, is what all men truly have in common with each other and with the whole of creation. Death is what you have essentially in common with me and the only reality, it seems, that we have in common with everyone else and everything else in this world.

Death, Evil, and Sin

Do not confuse death with either evil or sin, as is so often done, for example, in careless teaching and preaching in the churches. Death is to be carefully distinguished from both evil and sin. Each is related to the other, but they are different realities. For one thing, death is not the consequence of either evil or sin, nor is death some punishment for evil or sin.

Nor is there any such thing as objective evil, that is, some knowledge or idea or principle of evil which men can learn or discover or discern and then, by their own will, do evil or good. If men knew or could know what is good and what is evil in that sense, then they would be like God Himself.

But men are just men—not like God. Evil, in the sense in which men know of evil, exists only in some action, word, deed, or other happening that threatens the self-interest (not—notice—selfish interest, but self-interest, that is, welfare) of a person or institution or ideology or nation. Yet that which seems to be evil from the vantage of one *invariably* turns out to be good for some other. The terms *good* and *evil*, in this sense, and except when they are used to refer to the action of God in judging the world, have meaning relative to the self-interest of a person or country or whatever; they are not ultimate or abstract terms. What you or I might, in any given situation, think to be evil is always a very ambiguous and uncertain and partial insight, because what you or I can see of the situation—much less foresee of the consequences and final outcome of the situation—is limited, prejudiced, and identified with our own interest in our own lives and with the consequences that seem to affect our own lives.

That is why, in part, what seems to any man or nation to be good or evil can *never* be claimed by any man or nation to be the equivalent, or the content, or even the approximation of God's judgment, although men and nations constantly make just that pretense. They do so at their peril. They do so as a way of mocking God, as a way of making believe that they can second guess how God will judge their decisions or actions, as a way of asserting that they know already how God will judge themselves and others. That is perilous because *only a man who in fact does not believe in God* would so seriously usurp and absurdly challenge the freedom of God in judging all men and all things in all the world. That is an arrogant and a dangerous course because it is a way of playing God.

Indeed it is just this—the pretension to know already and beforehand how God judges and will judge human decisions and actions—that is the essence of sin. Sin is not essentially the mistaken, inadvertent, or deliberate choice of evil by men but the pride into which men fall in associating their own self-interest with the will of God. Sin is the denunciation of the freedom of God to judge men as it pleases Him to judge them. Sin is the displacement of God's will with one's own will. Sin is the radical confusion in men's lives as to whether God or man is morally sovereign in history. And those men who suppose that *they* are sovereign exist in acute estrangement in this history, separated from life itself and from the giver of life, from God. In that state, alienated from all of life, including their own life and the life of all others and all things, they are consigned to death, committed to the service of death, unable to save themselves from death.

Death is not the same reality as evil, but there is evil in death. That which is evil in death is the threat that death embodies of lost identity, of obliteration, of extinction, of the ruthless and final negation of self. There is evil in death, in this sense, because death is adverse to the most profound and elementary self-interest of a person or a society—the mere preservation of life.

Death and Youth

To some, I suppose, it may seem vulgar or irrelevant or otherwise inappropriate to write candidly about death, especially in a book addressed primarily to young people. The custom in America is not to mention death *even at funerals*. And least of all is death openly mentioned among or in front of the young, save when it is mentioned—if probably unheard and unheeded—in their baptisms. Yet death does not wait for full maturity and adulthood, for infirmity or age, for sickness or weakness to assail men. The work of death begins in the very moment of birth: death claims every man in the first consciousness of his existence. Death does not respect or wait upon the foolish amenities which cause men to hide from their offspring the truth that, for all the ingenuity and capability of men, death is present, powerful, and active in every moment, in every event and transaction of human experience.

No one is given birth who does not imminently confront the claim of death over his own life.

This is a book about death, and it is wholly appropriate that it is addressed to young people.

Is Death the Last Word?

Ironically, though death is so seldom frankly discussed between, say, parents and children, and though the meaning of death is clothed in superstition and myth, an underlying preoccupation with death is evident everywhere. The fear of death, especially the fear of one's own death, though sublimated, is the most universal dread men suffer.

The law, for example, is very much concerned with death, for the ultimate sanction of the law is the power of the state to take a man's life—and all the lesser penalties exacted by the law are symbols of this final sanction.

On the other hand, many people are fascinated and seem to be entertained by those who in the performing arts or in sports risk their lives, matching their own courage and skill against death, as circus performers or bullfighters or auto stunt drivers do. In literature and the other creative arts, a recurrent theme is death and the probing of the meaning of death in this life. Even in those seemingly corny and ridiculous old horror films—like *Frankenstein*—the issue is the presence and power of death in this world and the attempt— the unsane, sometimes insane, always futile attempt—of men to overcome the power of death.

Death is very much on the minds of men, and the mystery of death is given much attention by men, despite the conventional folkways in America that ban the mention of it in plain or personal language.

And do not laugh or scoff at the venerable images of the power of death named the Devil or the Angel of Death, for they are ways in which men have recognized that death is a living, active, decisive reality. And that is indeed what death is, however the face of death is visualized or portrayed. Such images of death are far more realistic and close to the truth than the modern superstitions that seek to avoid, put off, or altogether deny the vitality of death in daily life. Such images are wiser than the mythology associated with the meaning of death that regards death as if death were merely some destination, that is, as if death were remote from and abstract from today and every day, a reality only to be faced eventually, on some distant terminal day. Such images, too, are more discerning than the idea, popular nowadays, that death simply means biological extinction.

Death is all that, all right, but more than that: death is the contemporaneous power abrasively addressing every man in his own existence with the word that he is not only eventually and finally, but even now and already, estranged, separated, alienated, lost in his relationships with, at once, everybody and everything else, and— what is in a way much worse—his very own self. Death means total loss of identity.

Death, in *this* sense, death embodying this awful threat, is the death which is at work not only on the day of the undertaker, but today.

This is a book about death. It is, as well, a book about resurrection.

Of all the worldly powers, death is the most obvious, but death is not the greatest power active in the world. Death is not the last word. Nor is the last word some nebulous, fanciful, fake promise of an after life. If you have been told or taught anything such as that in church, what you have heard is heresy. The last word is not death, nor life after death, but the last word is the same as the first word, and *that* word is Jesus Christ. He has, holds, and exercises power even over death in this world. And His promise is that a man may be set free from bondage to death in this life here and now.

2

Loneliness, Dread, and Holiness

> *Three times I besought the Lord about this, that
> it should leave me; but he said to me, "My
> grace is sufficient for you, for my power is made
> perfect in weakness. . . ."*
>
> II Corinthians 12:8–9

LONELINESS is as intimate and as common to men as death.

Loneliness does not respect persons, but afflicts all—men and
women, those of status and the derelicts, the adolescents and the
old people, the single and the married, the learned and the illiterate,
and, one might add, the clergy and the laity.

It is an ordinary affliction, though perhaps more noticed and
more readily admitted among some than others—among those, for
instance, whose loneliness becomes so desperate as to be pathological, or among those forgotten by society in prisons or hospitals or
boweries, or among both older and younger single folk.

Loneliness is more evident in the city, or so it seems to be,
since the largest group of people now migrating to the city are no
longer distinguished by nationality or race but by the fact that they
are single. These migrants are mainly young people—students or recent graduates, artists and professionals, white-collar workers of all
sorts—coming to the city to work and live and look for each other.
Taken with the older people of the city—the widowed and the retired—they make single people a very substantial part of the urban
population.

That the proportion of young single people in the city is greater
than elsewhere does not prove that loneliness is any more prevalent
in the city, but it is perhaps more apparent in the city, and the fictions that attach to the escape from loneliness are perchance pursued

and practiced more publicly and more frantically in the city. The very size of the city, not to mention the variety and versatility of the city's life, promises at best some therapy for loneliness and at least some distraction from it.

Loneliness is the specific apprehension of a person of his own death in relation to the impending death of all men and all things. Loneliness is the experience in which the fear of a man of his own personal death coincides with his fright of the death of everyone and everything else. Loneliness is not a unique or an isolated experience; on the contrary, it is the ordinary but still overwhelming anxiety that all relationships are lost. Loneliness does not deny or negate the existence of lives other than the life of the one who is lonely, but loneliness so vividly anticipates the death of such other lives that they are of no sustenance or comfort to the life and being of the one who suffers loneliness.

Loneliness is the most caustic, drastic, and fundamental repudiation of God. Loneliness is the most elementary expression of original sin.

There is no man who does not know loneliness.

Yet there is no man who is alone.

Fictions of Loneliness

This subject is too profoundly subjective to pretend to be very analytical about it, but some of the fictions associated with loneliness can be identified even though they cannot be sharply distinguished.

. . . that it is unfilled time

One fiction is that loneliness is contingent upon time, that loneliness essentially means unfilled or unused time. Loneliness is thought to be a vacuum in which one exists between periods of occupation in work or play, or in the absence of companions. Loneliness, here, is the experience of void.

Many persons just work to death, at first in school activities, either studies or extracurricular work, and later on in some job. They leave school or job only to sleep alone or eat alone, and they try in their work—whatever it be—to remain so occupied and preoccupied that the empty time is filled.

The void may be mere boredom, that is, activity for the sake of using up surplus time because of a shortage of school activities or other work or play or companionship. The exploitation of boredom in the city, the supply of things to do and places to go in order just to spend leftover time, is organized commercially in an elaborate fashion. Dance studios catering to both young and old, health salons and gyms, clubs engaged in acquainting people with each other, private parties to which invitations can be purchased, sometimes church youth groups—all of these, and many more, traffic in boredom and profit in one way or another from promising that time will be consumed for those who pay the price or put up with other requirements.

Some people, young as well as old, never get around to spending their boredom in the presence of others, but spend it physically alone gazing at whatever happens to appear on their television set or entranced with the noise of a transistor radio. It is as if the sight or sound of other human beings, without any direct or serious involvement with them, were enough to prove that they are not alone.

Even popular dancing avoids involvement with others nowadays and becomes a solitary exercise with many characteristics of a fantasy experience in which you twist and contort and burlesque your own body but never touch or hold or embrace your partner and, in fact, just dance alone, as if beguiled with the thought of involvement but still afraid to become involved.

Meanwhile, on every corner of the city is a bar—not now the elegant places which cater to the transient lonely, but the little, cruddy neighborhood taverns, the kind that can also be found in almost any small town—in which, night after night, sit side by side on rows of stools the very same people who live side by side in the same block or building, exchanging boredom for oblivion.

For those as yet not old enough—or old enough looking—to drink there is instead a hangout on the corner—a candy store or soda fountain or hamburger joint—where one can find some privacy from parents and teachers (if not from cops) and get lost in the noise of the jukebox or in the anonymity of a gang.

If you will, of course, you can patronize more esoteric establishments with special clienteles—prostitutes or homosexuals or gamblers or whatever one wants—and there relieve loneliness in lust and chance.

. . . that it can be satisfied in erotic infatuation

These are places often populated by those who realize that loneliness is more than the burden of time and who are beguiled by another fiction—that loneliness is satisfied in erotic infatuation.

Here are people, whether men or women, whether boys or girls, whether looking for the same or the other sex, for whom seduction finally becomes a way of life. Here are people insisting upon the importance of what meets the eye or other senses: external impressions, physique, cosmetics, the appearances of youth.

Here are the lonely whose search for some partner is so dangerous, so stimulating, and so exhausting that the search itself provides an apparent escape from loneliness. But when the searching stops, when a partner is found for an hour or a night or an affair, the search immediately resumes. The searching becomes compulsive. And while erotic companionship seems more appealing—and more human—than resignation to boredom, while touching each other may be more intimate and more honest than watching each other, no one may really overcome his loneliness, find his own identity, in another, least of all in the body of another.

. . . that it can be answered in possession

Perhaps that is the most absurd fiction of them all: the notion, present, primitively, in erotic partnerships, *but also very often in other relationships—between parents and children, in friendship, in marriage*—that the answer to loneliness, that one's own identity, must be sought and is to be found in another person. This is, of course, an idea of venerable origin—the early Greeks thought man and woman are two halves in pursuit of a whole person to be found in their joinder. It is also an idea of contemporary popularity: think, for example, of the ridiculous idealism of much instruction about "Christian marriage," or think of the erotica disguised and presented on television and through other mass media.

To pursue and take one's own identity from the person of another is to equate love with possession. Fits of jealousy are inevitable in any such liaison, for each time the other's attention or affection is drawn to somebody else, the one whose identity is taken from that other's life is damaged. At worst the fiction that one's identity is to be found in another is cannibalistic—a devouring of another; at best it is a possessive, if romantic, manipulation by one of another in the name of love.

Loneliness as a Foretaste of Death

None of these fictions significantly addresses the experience of loneliness, none is more than an illusory comfort for the lonely. Separately or together they are omens of the very reality of which loneliness is the foretaste: *death*. How then could any of them have power to answer loneliness? How could any do other than dramatize loneliness all the more? Is there any answer to loneliness?

Will you look for release in your work? It can fill the time but not the void. Work is the estrangement of men from the rest of creation. Work—as it is discussed later in this book—means the bondage of men to the rest of creation, a sign of death, as great a burden to men as the isolation of men from each other which is time.

Will you turn then to leisure? Foolish men, leisure is merely another word for work, embodying the same animosity between men and the rest of creation. Leisure, or non-work in any of its other forms, is as much an anticipation of death as work.

Perhaps another drink will help. Maybe a drink will induce you to forget that this loneliness is not the absence of others, but your presence among others when your presence is treated as absence. Perhaps another drink will help you to forget that you are regarded as if you are dead. Perhaps another drink will let you forget you are forgotten.

Get some sex. If you find some, maybe you will find yourself too. If you find some, at least you will not be alone, though you will still be lonely. And if, after awhile, you have no luck in finding either sex or yourself, your fatigue in the search will overcome both your desire and your need, and then, at least, you will be able to sleep alone again long enough to wake refreshed to resume the search. Live in the consolation of looking for what you need where it surely cannot be found and you will always harbor, if nothing else, a little false hope. That is the way to die.

See a psychiatrist. You cannot cope with loneliness alone. Maybe, if you search yourself and your biography with a doctor's patience, you can find something or someone to blame yourself upon. Anyway, you can explain your anxieties to him, even if he cannot absolve you of any guilt. Perhaps he can help you to abide your own death, even though he cannot save you from it.

Maybe you will find a lover. Any face that passes on the street might be your lover. Do you wonder how you look to those who pass? Do they wonder the same of you? Dare you speak? Or make any gesture? If you do, they may turn away. They may murder you when all you want is their love. No. Loneliness is more familiar than annihilation, and thus seems more secure. Better stay where you are.

Try marriage. It is the more sensible course. You ought to be able to make a go of it. Lots have. No more returning to an empty room; there will be another to share the emptiness. And, who knows? There may be more to share than that. Your better half may be the part of you that's missing. You may discover who you are in your mate, or, failing that, in your offspring, and that would after all be better than dying as you are, alone.

Be more positive! Now there's a thought. Defeat your loneliness by affirming that it does not exist. Hypnotize yourself. Make believe, as children do, and it will seem, for a little while, just as you pretend, until, of course, the rueful day when you realize that things are not as bad as they seem only because, in fact, they seem as bad as they are.

End it now. This living is not life. It is death. Why not salute the fact and dramatize it? Wherever you turn you see the face of death: all these disguises do not hide *that* face. All these temptations are emissaries of death. The presence of death is hidden everywhere, the power of death is awful. Why not find out how great death is? End it all now. If death is so great then this foretaste of death, this loneliness, will be ended in death, too. Then you won't be lonely anymore. Then you won't be.

Poor you! Pity yourself: everybody else does. Loathe the fact that you cannot remember who you are and so no one else can

19

recognize you. Hate—hate is a form of pity—the fact that you are someone other than the one you wish to be, other than the one you imagine would earn the love of others. (You idiot! Love cannot be earned. No one deserves a gift, else where's the act of giving? Love is volunteered, and if you do not know that you are loved, it is not you who are rejected, it is you who are repudiating the one who loves you. Pity yourself for that.)

Pray. It is a last resort, I know. Still, nothing else dispels this gruesome desolation. But how do you do it? That's just the trouble, friend. Prayer is nothing you do, prayer is someone you are. Prayer is not about doing, but being. Prayer is about being alone in God's presence. Prayer is being *so* alone that God is the only witness to your existence. The secret of prayer is God affirming your life. To be *that* alone is incompatible with loneliness. In prayer you cannot be lonely. It *is* the last resort.

The Surrender to Death and the Triumph of Grace

There is no man who does not know loneliness: even Jesus Christ. He did not succumb to loneliness because there is no man who is alone.

On the face of the Gospel narrative is the lonely Christ. Nobody greeted, nobody honored, nobody understood, nobody loved, nobody celebrated His vocation. Nobody loved Him for being the One He is.

In His birth He was sought as an earthly ruler. He suffered the rebuke of Mary and Joseph when, as a child, He was found in the Temple in discourse with the teachers. When He submitted to baptism, He bewildered a protesting John the Baptist. It was rejection He experienced when His relatives called on Him to name them in preference to the crowd. He healed the sick, but both sick and well mistook His power. When He spoke in the Temple, He was not heard or heeded. The same temptations that visited Him in the wilderness returned to taunt Him in the political triumph of Palm Sunday, and His own disciples were—and many are to this very day—astonished and perplexed that He withstood such attractive temptations. Israel, which had boasted in her waiting for His coming, found Him subversive when He came. Rome was an accomplice in His condemnation. At Gethsemane, while He was alone in prayer, His friends slept and His enemies plotted to destroy Him. Judas betrayed Him, Peter denied Him, all the rest fled. A thief ridiculed Him on the Cross. The people shouted for His death.

Unwelcome, misunderstood, despised, rejected, unloved and mis-loved, condemned, betrayed, deserted, helpless—He was delivered to death as if He were alone.

Christ descended into hell: Christ is risen from death.

In the submission of Christ to death, the power of death is dis-sipated. In the subjection of Christ to death, the dread is taken out of loneliness. Christ suffered loneliness without despair. In the radi-cal loneliness of Christ is the assurance that no man is alone.

In surrender to death, in hell, in the event in which the presence and power of death is most notorious, undisguised, militant, and per-vasive, the reality and grace of God are triumphant.

In the event in which you are alone with your own death— when all others and all things are absent and gone—God's initiative affirms your very creation and that you are given your life anew. In the moment and place where God is least expected—in the barren-ness and emptiness of death—God is at hand.

It is in that event that a man discovers it is death which is alone, not he.

Loneliness and the Ethics of Holiness

There is no man who does not know loneliness, even Jesus Christ. But Christ Himself has shown that there is no man who is alone.

You are not alone. Do not be so proud any more of your lone-liness. It is only the shadow of your death, and your death, your loneliness, is like the death of every other man. But your death is overpowered in the patience of God's love for you. Your fear that you are not loved does not negate the gift which God's love is. Your loneliness does not avoid God's love, it only repudiates His love for you. You cannot flee from God's pres-ence. You are not alone.

Now you are free. You are free from the idol your own death becomes in loneliness. You are free from all the frantic escapes, free from trying to purchase love, free from anonymity. You are free now from searching, because you have been found. You are free. Your life is found in the life of God. You are not alone.

Now you can love. Love yourself. That is the rudiment of all other loves. Love yourself: that means your final acceptance of and active participation in God's love of you. Love yourself. If you love yourself you will become and be one who can love another. Love yourself and then your love of others will be neither suicidal nor destructive, neither jealous nor possessive, but then your love of yourself will enable, embody, enrich, and elucidate your love of others, and your other loves will do the same to your self-love. And when you love others—tell them so—celebrate it—not only by some words but by your life toward them and toward the whole of the world. Your specific love of another is verified and supported in your love of all others and all things, even those or that which seem to be unlovable, which seem unworthy to be loved. Let that be the manner of your witness to the One who loves all though none are worthy, not even one. You are not alone.

Don't be afraid. There is no more to fear. Do not fear rejection. If you fear rejection by another you do not love the other, though you may profess it. You are only being anxious for his love of you. The free man does not seek the love of others, nor fear that his love will be rejected, for rejection—as is known from the night in which Christ was betrayed—does not destroy love, and it does not destroy the one who loves. Don't be afraid, you are not alone.

Now you are whole. Your work and the time you spend not working now both become sacraments of the solidarity between yourself and the rest of creation, sacraments of the reconciliation wrought, for you, by Christ. Now work and leisure become virtually indistinguishable from worship, that is, from the enjoyment of God's love not just for you, but for all, including those who do not yet enjoy God's love for themselves or for anyone or anything else.

The enjoyment of God in this way is, of course, the estate of holiness. Holiness does not mean that you are any better than anyone else; holiness is not the same as goodness; holiness is not common piety. Holiness is not about pleasing God, even less about appeasing God. Holiness is about enjoying God. Holiness is the integrity of greeting, confessing, honoring, and trusting God's presence in all events and in any event, no matter what, no matter when, no matter where.

Therefore, rejoice:
Reckon your weakness as praise of God's power, endure suffering in joy, risk your life on the veracity of Christ, count your loneliness a means of grace.

3

Sex and the Search for Self

> *Now concerning the unmarried, I have no com-*
> *mand of the Lord, but I give my opinion as one*
> *who by the Lord's mercy is trustworthy.*
>
> I Corinthians 7:25

IN SEX, whatever the species or practice, the issue is not pleasure or lust, but personal identity.

Sex is by no means the only way in which the quest for personal identity is pursued. The same may be sought in daily work or the upbringing of children, in that for which one spends money, in sports, in study even, or in the practice of the arts. Whatever the case in these other realms, the search for self is the most prevalent aspect of sex.

The discovery of self, or, more precisely, the recovery of self—the gift of personal identity—is, at the same time, the very theme of the Gospel. Christ is, pre-eminently, the man who knows what it is to be a human being. Christ is the true image of man amidst a people who do not know what it is to be fully human, amidst those, including His own family and His disciples, who are profoundly troubled about their own identities and both wondrously attracted to and pathetically threatened by His presence. They do not know who they are as persons for the very reason that they have not yet recognized who He is.

It is not possible to consider sex seriously in terms of the search for self without sooner or later confronting the promise of the Gospel that the secret of personal identity for *every* person is found in Christ. It is just this—what it means to be human—that is the essential content of what the Gospel has to say about sex. It is this and not the conventional denunciations, heard in so many churches, of sex as sin or of sex as something foul or dirty or animalistic. It is this and not surrender to the temptation to suppress sex and the subject of sex in the churches or, what is worse, the more common temptation to condone sex as long as it is discreetly practiced and condemn sex only when it becomes a matter of ordinary scandal.

In other words, it is quite all right to mention sex in the sanctuary—as it is also appropriate to speak within the church of any other matter that occupies the attentions of men in the world. The life and action within the sanctuary has integrity only insofar as it is concerned with and encompasses the life that takes place outside the sanctuary. Nothing that has ever been said or done in a bedroom, in the back seat of a car, or, for that matter, in a brothel, is beyond the scope of the Gospel, and, therefore, beyond the Church's care for the world. The fantasies, fears, and fairy tales associated with sex must be dispelled so that within the Church sex is admitted, discussed, and understood with intelligence, maturity, compassion, and, most of all, a reverence for the ministry of Christ in restoring human life to men.

Sex and the Sanctuary

Especially among youth, sex is commonly treated in the churches as if it does not seriously exist or as if it ought not seriously to exist before or outside of marriage. Thus the Church generally ignores the fact that sex is a profoundly influential reality in the daily lives of young people. Kids are afflicted too much in church youth conferences and Sunday schools and youth fellowships with presentations about "marriage and the family" that offer only simplified, idealized, foolish, and often false images of sex, and which treat sex as an obligation exclusive to marriage and procreation. At the same time, these presentations shun or merely deplore the immediate sexual issues confronting young people who, according to the realities of modern American life, are practically—that is, economically and educationally, if not psychologically and physiologically—unable to marry for many more years—after school or college, after military service, after landing a job, after saving some money, after a long while.

Meanwhile, the immediate sexual problems and questions that commonly assail young people are more often than not neglected, unmentioned, and even considered unmentionable, their existence, in effect, denied: petting and fondling, premarital and extramarital intercourse, masturbation, homosexuality, sexual adjustment in relationships with parents and teachers and other adults, and the mystery of sex and love.

It does not contribute to the nurture of adolescents, nor does it enhance the prospects of a mature and stable adulthood, to confront young people with an ideal of so-called Christian marriage that is beyond the possibility of prompt, practical fulfillment for them.

More than that, it would be more healthy, human, and honest for churchpeople, instead of dwelling so exclusively on the image of marriage, to distinguish the varieties of sexual experiment and sex acts, on the one hand, and the fact of sexuality on the other, and then to admit to themselves and to youth that *all* relationships are, in some sense and to some degree, sexual: between a man and his wife, of course, but also between parent and child, friend and friend, one and another wherever they meet, whatever their gender. Sexuality is an aspect of every human transaction or communication, though nothing may happen to dramatize the fact, and though in any relationship it is *never* the sole reality. The sexuality of all persons should cause it to be recognized how common sexual activity is, how familiar it is in one way or another to everybody and how, therefore, it is a matter which cannot ever be effectively ignored or suppressed. (Indeed the suppression of sex, the refusal or fear of discussing the actualities of sex, the denial of the ordinary sexuality of persons, are all in fact sexual acts, though they be somewhat perverse ones.) Sexuality is universal. Sex is mundane. That is reason enough that sex be dealt with candidly and realistically within the Church.

The Notion of Christian Marriage

Acknowledging all this might also enable the truth to be faced that there really is no such thing as "Christian marriage," as the term is commonly used. "Christian marriage" is a vain, romantic, unbiblical conception. "Christian marriage" is a fiction. There is no more an institution of "Christian marriage" than there is a "Christian nation" or a "Christian lawyer" or a "Christian athlete." Even where such terms are invoked as a matter of careless formulation and imprecise speech, they are symptoms of a desire to separate Christians from the common life of the world, whereas Christians are called into radical involvement in the common life of the world. To be sure, there are Christians who are athletes and those who practice law, and there are Christians who are citizens of this and the other nations, but none of these or similar activities or institutions are in any respect essentially Christian, nor can they be changed or reconstituted in order to become Christian. They are, on the contrary, realities of the fallen life of the world; they are inherently secular, worldly, subject to the power of death, aspects of the present, transient, perishing existence of the world. It is the same with marriage. Marriage is a fallen estate, which, remember, does not mean that it is not an honorable estate but only means it is a relationship subject to death, a relationship appropriate for and only established in the present age, but not known, or, more precisely, radically transcended and transfigured in both the Creation and the Eschaton, in both the beginning and the end of human history.

As with any other reality of secular life, the Christian takes marriage seriously for what it is, but for no more nor any less than that. The Christian does not suffer illusions about marriage, but recognizes that marriage is, in the first instance, a civil contract in which two parties promise to exchange certain services and responsibilities with respect to each other and to assume certain obligations for offspring of the marriage. At the same time, marriage is no merely private contract, for society at large has a particular interest in the honoring and enforcement of this contract. If the marriage contract is observed and performed with reasonable diligence, society generally, as well as the married couple and their children, benefits since an enduring marriage contributes to the economic, social, and psychological stability of the whole of society.

The fiction that there is some ideal of marriage for Christians which is better than or essentially different from the ordinary secular marriage is not only fostered by most Sunday school curriculum materials on the subject, but also by the practice of authorizing the clergy to act for the state in the execution of the marriage contract. Clergymen are licensed by the state to perform the functions of a civil magistrate in marriage, in spite of the supposed separation of church and state in this country. This both lends weight to the confusion about "Christian marriage," and greatly compromises the discretion of the clergy as to whom they shall marry. In the office and function of a civil magistrate, no clergyman really has the grounds to refuse to marry any couple who present themselves to him, whether they are Christians or not, whether they are temperamentally or otherwise ready to marry, as long as they meet the civil requirements for marriage, that is, are of certain ages, have had blood tests, meet any residence requirements, have a valid license, and pay the fee.

A more theologically responsible practice, I suggest, would be to divest the clergy of this civil office and require that all who will be married present themselves to the civil magistrate to be married. Then, if those who are so married are Christians, they will go to their congregation to offer, within the company of the Church, their marriage to be blessed, to seek the intercessions of the whole Church for the marriage, and to celebrate their marriage in the Church as a sacrament. In fact, of course, a similar practice is followed in many parts of Europe and Latin America.

To restore such a practice would go a long way toward recovering the sacramental integrity of marriage between Christians. For to discard the fiction of "Christian marriage" and to understand that marriage is an ordinary, secular, and fallen estate in no way denigrates marriage for Christians. On the contrary, the Christian is, in marriage and everything else, fully participant in secular life, but at the same time he is constantly engaged in offering his involvement in secular life for the glory of God. In such an offering, that which is ordinary is rendered extraordinary, that which is merely worldly is transfigured, that which is most common becomes the means of worship, and each act or event of everyday life becomes sacramental: a sign and celebration of God's care for every act and event of everyday life in this world. Rather than demean or downgrade marriage, to restore such a practice would give again to the marriages of Christians the dignity of that which is secular made holy, of that which is a sign of death become a witness to redemption to all those, married or not, who are not Christian.

Sex and Society

The confusion about the meaning of marriage is very modest compared to that associated with sexual acts or experiences prior to or outside of marriage, such as premarital and extramarital intercourse, masturbation, petting, homosexuality, and so on, though these are matters of more immediate and constant concern to most young people. The churches have treated these matters too occasionally, too superficially, and too piously.

It is of first importance to acknowledge that no man is the judge of any other man, nor is a man even his own judge, nor is society the judge, nor, least of all, is the Church the judge of any man.

Each man and every man, this society and all societies, the Church and the churches—all are judged in the event of the Word of God and in no other way are they judged.

Society is not the judge, but society does seek to preserve itself and, for the sake of that, through law or custom, to condone conduct that is deemed socially beneficial and to condemn conduct that is deemed detrimental to the peace and welfare of society. But keep in mind, as the Church of England has authoritatively recognized, that what society determines from time to time to be criminal or otherwise antisocial behavior is not synonymous with sin.

Society generally condemns as criminally antisocial, sexual acts involving coercion of one by another, or involving a public nuisance, or endangering a breach of the peace. However, under the impact of the more recent insights of psychiatry and psychology, the law tends to consider acts such as these as symptomatic of illness rather than of criminal intent and therefore more appropriately treated medically than by confinement in prison.

In other specific circumstances, sexual conduct may not violate any criminal statutes or even be sensibly or justifiably classified as criminal, but nonetheless constitute antisocial behavior and therefore suffer the moral censure of society. This is so, for example, where conduct tends to undermine the integrity and stability and performance of the marriage contract, as in the case of extramarital intercourse and perhaps most, but not necessarily all, incidents of premarital intercourse; in incestuous relations between parents and children—which are, incidentally, far more common than is generally conceded—and in some homosexual liaisons, like those where one of the partners is married.

Obviously, certain forms of sexual behavior are not intrinsically antisocial, although some particular sexual act in a specific instance may represent a form of personal hostility toward society, or nonconformity, or maladjustment to society, or simply illness. The test for society and for the law is whether, in the specific case, the act engaged in has consequences adverse to the peace and welfare of society generally. But where it appears that the consequences of the particular conduct are significant only or mainly to those immediately involved in the conduct, society has insufficient interest in the conduct to take notice of it, much less legally or morally to censure it.

The consequences of any action or event can never be fully anticipated or calculated, but that does not relieve society from discriminating among those situations which bluntly and fiercely threaten the common welfare and safety of society, and those which, as far as can be predicted or analyzed, do not. Thus, sexual conduct involving coercion or duress—like rape—is fitly declared a crime because it so radically endangers human life and is so frequently associated with other extreme, antisocial, often pathological, behavior —such as murder or theft. On the other hand, if two unmarried adults in good health, with sensible precautions, in the privacy of a home, by mutual consent, spend a night together, the consequences of such an encounter that can be foreseen are so personal and private, pertain so exclusively to the two involved, that society's interest in their conduct should not be asserted to invade their privacy or to censor or curtail their conduct or—least of all—to judge or punish it.

In other words, in any of the realms of sex, society must consider not only the externals—the acts committed or performed—but the persons involved in those acts—their ages and sexes and maturity and other relationships—and, for that matter, all the other aspects of the specific incident.

Sex and Adolescence

Consider, now, the varieties of sexual conduct most characteristic of adolescent life, conduct which is not *intrinsically* antisocial—although in some given instance it may in fact be antisocial or may conceal a latent antisocial problem.

. . . petting

Probably, one might add normatively, the most typical sexual conduct of adolescents is that discovery, exploration, and enjoyment of sexuality which is evident in heavy necking, petting, and fondling. Such conduct, I suggest, is not in itself antisocial. But where these preliminary, customary, and inherited rituals of sex (so widely, by the way, displayed in public media—in movies and television, in advertising and in magazines—and so much exhibited in the examples of adults), arouse imminent desire or necessity for sexual climax, they are fraught with great perils. These perils include illegitimate births, habituation to a peculiar sexual exercise, the impossibility of marriage—for the time being for the particular couple —grave frustrations or the oppressions of guilt, disloyalties to others or the abuse of one's sexual partner. Perils such as these counsel caution in, though they do not forbid, the practices of petting and the like so common in adolescent life.

As a practical matter, however, these perils do not appear to be effective deterrents to adolescent sexual promiscuity. Venereal disease, illegitimate births, and forced marriages because of pregnancies continue to increase greatly both in the city and in the schools and communities outside the city. The ways in which solicitation for intercourse by a boy of a girl or by a girl of a boy are common knowledge, at least to adolescents if not to their parents, teachers, or pastors. If a boy, for example, invites a girl to a drive-in movie, she is often accepting an invitation for hot necking and fondling and, more often than not, for intercourse. If a girl wears certain insignia (usually a pin or some other piece of jewelry, though the items vary in different places and change frequently as they become publicly notorious) she is advertising either her experience in or desire for experience in sex. And both boy and girl homosexual youths have their own signals and insignia.

Where such are the mores of adolescent society, it is hard for an individual boy or girl to resist conforming to that which everyone else says and does, whether they really want to or not. Conformity here, just as in many other segments of American life, is thought to be synonymous with popularity or at least to be the purchase price of popularity. Yet, in the very nature of the case, mere conformity is a violence to one's person and personality.

Who are you if you are just like everybody else? I will tell you plainly who you are—*you are nobody!* If you are a conformist, just for the sake of being that, it is as if you did not exist in any significant, personal, or human way whatever. It is no real popularity that you gain if your own personality is suffocated in the effort to conform. *You* cannot be popular, much less accepted and loved—

which involves a different thing than simple popularity—if you are anonymous, and yet it is exactly anonymity into which conformity invites you. If you are a conformist, if you look and act and talk like everybody else, you are nobody, and, if you are nobody, you might as well be dead in fact since you are already dead in principle.

... cosmetics and clothing

Nowhere, I suppose, is the tyranny of conformity more obvious in American society than in the use of cosmetics and in the fashions of clothing.

Cosmetics are by no means a modern invention or custom. Both men and women have from primitive times used various paints and pigments and perfumes to adorn their bodies. Cosmetics are one of the inherited rituals of human life, associated, by the way, not only with sex *per se*, but with class and caste, office, status, wealth, station. Where the uses of cosmetics are not corrupted (as they are in America) they serve to indicate some sort of position in society or to enhance the beauty of the human body. Of course opinions vary in different societies as to what enhances the beauty of the body. In some societies what would be thought attractive might in another be thought ugly or mutilating. But in our society cosmetics are increasingly used—by both women and men—to serve the ideal of mass conformity, to make everybody look like everybody else. Usually the standards of conformity in such matters are identified with some public idol such as a movie star or other public figure, and therefore they tend to create a deception. Conformity in the uses of cosmetics is so common and extenuated that it is like dating a person who is engaged in imitating somebody else, whether that is the intention or the result. There is a great obstacle to actually meeting, much less loving, the real person hidden under the mask. It would, I guess, be nice to date Elizabeth Taylor, but it is not very interesting to date Sally Jones when she is disguised as Elizabeth Taylor, for, in that case, I will end up being with neither Elizabeth Taylor nor Sally Jones, but only with some mannequin.

The same problems are related to clothing fashions, but added to them, ironically, is the increasing tendency among adolescents, but not exclusively among them, for clothes to obscure the sexual identity of the person. At least in the city, it becomes more and more difficult to distinguish girls from boys or boys from girls according to how they dress. The fashions of each sex are remarkably similar, each imitative of the other, and this raises the issue of how much Americans are becoming at one and the same time a most sexually conscious people, but also a sexless people who have lost a sense of both what it means to be masculine and what it means to be feminine.

I do not purpose to speculate about why this might be the case in America, or whether it is an especially American problem. I simply observe that, in an atmosphere in which Americans are increasingly indoctrinated into the same ideas, attitudes, and practices of all sorts, conformity is also at work in making boys and girls and men and women more and more indistinguishable—at least in their outward appearance.

. . . pornography

The conformities in the uses of both cosmetics and clothing are probably indications both of the suppression of sexuality and of the profound insecurity among young people and others as to their sexual identity. But a word should be added about another form of sexual suppression which has wide currency among adolescents in America: pornography.

Pornographic pictures and literature, of course, should not be confused with erotica. As the courts both in England and America have repeatedly held, erotica is the artistically significant portrayal, pictorially or verbally, of the reality, integrity, and beauty of sexual relationships. Pornography, in contrast, portrays abnormal or atypical sexual activity in a fashion that is provocative, dehumanizing, and obscene. Pornography and pseudopornography are very easily accessible to and widely circulated among young people nowadays and have the proportions of a major commercial enterprise. There are questions for society and the law to consider about how this traffic can be controlled in order that it not mislead or corrupt young people, without at the same time destroying the civil rights of both those who market and those who purchase pornography.

But the more important question for us may have to do with why pornographic materials have such a ready market among youth. Part of the matter surely is the very secrecy, the clandestine nature, of receiving such materials. And part of it is, I suppose, just curiosity about sex which is whetted by discussions of sex and by the sublimation of sexual conduct at the behest of parents or church. If sex in all of its meanings, practices, and rituals is not in the open—frankly recognized, intelligently considered, and compassionately dealt with—then what is to be expected except that sex will be the subject of gossip, rumor, escapism, fantasy, and the lure of that which is forbidden? Recourse to pornography among adolescents is, as far as I can discern, far less the consequence of racketeer activities or abnormal adolescent preoccupation with sex than of the fear of candor about sex among adults, including parents and pastors.

. . . masturbation

Another common—in fact virtually universal—variety of sexual experience characteristic of adolescent life is masturbation. Here, too, there is nothing inherently antisocial in the act. But one who persists into adulthood in the practice of masturbation is likely to be one who remains profoundly immature sexually, fearing actual sexual contact with a partner, becoming and being sexually retarded. The main danger and damage in masturbation is not in the conduct itself, but in the fantasy life that invariably accompanies the conduct. That life will hardly ever be a sexually identifying and fulfilling one, and indeed masturbation is probably most obviously another variety of sexual sublimation, one in which the sexual identity and capability of the person remains stalemated, indefinite, confused, and apparently self-contained. Masturbation is not *per se* antisocial, but the deep suppression of sexuality which it represents will frequently provoke some other, superficially nonsexual, antisocial behavior. And even if the sublimation of masturbation is never relieved, either in sexual relationship with another human being or in some antisocial, apparently nonsexual, behavior, the real tragedy—the destructive and dehumanizing fact about masturbation—is its obvious unfulfillment and crude futility among the varieties of sexual activity.

. . . homosexuality

Perhaps no sexual issue in American society among adolescents, although also among adults, both male and female, is more the subject of superstition, rejection, gossip, and uncouth humor than homosexuality. And, although petting and masturbation seldom come to the attention of the legal authorities (though much to the attention of parents and teachers), homosexuality is often a concern of the law. As in some other cases—notably, in my own experience as a lawyer, in narcotics addiction cases—the law regarding homosexuality is very much behind the insights of the medical sciences as to the understanding or treatment of it either personally or socially. In the law the term is loosely used to designate a fantastically diverse range of sexual conduct and identity. Everything from transvestitism, which is a complex and perplexing ailment, to the most casual sexual contact between two youths of the same sex, a contact provoked by curiosity or immaturity, not by compulsion, illness, or physiological disorder, this whole range and variety of sexual life is indiscriminately and unfairly and stupidly lumped together, and very often dealt with by the law as if it were all the same phenomenon.

Some of the confusion in the law, if not in the public mind, about what homosexuality is has begun to be dispelled by the readiness of the courts in many jurisdictions to heed medical authority as to the treatment rather than the imprisonment of those charged with criminal offenses involving homosexuality.

In spite of this enlightenment, many, perhaps essentially among churchpeople, will still find homosexual relations personally incomprehensible, aesthetically abhorrent, and morally reprehensible. Be that as it may, more fundamental issues than those of personal distaste are involved in the practice of homosexuality. Homosexuals are often tempted to suicide, experience desperate identity crises, sometimes are victims of extortion or blackmail, live in fear of exposure and social disgrace, suffer much from profound and unabsolved guilt, are readily vulnerable to venereal disease, feel more persecuted than other social minorities, perhaps have endured the collapse of relationships with parents and families, may—despite lots of sex—have never known love. These are the significant personal and social issues of homosexuality.

Sex and Sin

In all the varieties of sexual conduct, let it be repeated emphatically that none of the acts of sex which society in one way or another from time to time regards as criminal, or in some lesser degree antisocial, is thereby necessarily also to be regarded as sin. Contrariwise, those forms of conduct that do not fall under the censure, legally or morally, of society are not by that fact to be assumed to be free of sin. Society is not the judge of any man's sin.

Remember, too, that the Biblical description of sin is not so much the designation of certain kinds of conduct as sin—in sex or in any other realm of human life—as it is the usurpation by men of the prerogative of God in judging all human decisions and actions. Every specific act—every thought, word, and deed—of every person, and, as well, of every institution and nation, is subject to *that* judgment, and *that* judgment is in no wise mitigated, altered, or influenced by the opinions of men, or any man, or society as to that which is in truth good or evil. Or, to put it a bit differently, the Christian knows and confesses that in all things—in every act and decision—men are sinners and that in no way, by any ingenuity, piety, sanction, or social conformity, may a man escape from the full burden of the power of sin over his whole existence.

If you remember that the self-interest of society in condemning certain conduct is to be distinguished from sin, and that God Himself is the judge and there is none other, and that in no matter is any person pure from sin, then you can have some insight into the reality of sin in sex. That which is sinful in a radical sense in sexual behavior is the failure, refusal, or incapacity to acknowledge and treat your own self or another or both as persons. Sin essentially is the state of existence in which the separation of a person from God means his own loss of identity and the forfeiture of his relationship with other persons, and, in fact, with the whole rest of creation. Sin is consignment to death: to be cut off from the One in whom all life originates and in whom all life is fulfilled, to be, in fact, cut off from life itself. The power of sin permeates the rituals of sex, in all their varieties—in marriage and out of marriage, among young or old, among male and female—just as it does in all other affairs in this world. Thus it becomes and is a tribute to death, a sign of the imminence of death in this life.

Concretely, of course, the vitality of sin in sex is seen in situations where manipulation, punishment, humiliation, or violation of one by another or of one by one's own self is made obvious because of physical or psychological coercion, or of willful enticement, or of false promises, or fraud, or of the exchange of money or other consideration, or of lust or possessiveness. However, the dishonoring of the body and person of one's self or another may take subtle forms and may be as much present in sexual conduct approved or condoned by society as in that which is disapproved or condemned.

Yet the Christian more than recognizes the reality of sin in sex of all sorts. He knows, beyond that, that this—sex—which is so full of death, may also become and be a sacrament of the redemption of human life from the power of sin which death is.

Sex and the Search for Self

Such is the mystery of sex and love that what in sex may be dehumanizing, or merely habitual, or even depraved, may become human, sacramental, and sanctified. For sex to be so great an event as that, it is essential for a person to know who he is as a person, to be secure in his own identity, and, indeed, to love himself.

Too commonly sex does not have the dignity of a sacramental event because sex is thought to be the means of the search for self rather than the expression and communication of one who has already found himself, and is free from resort to sex in the frantic pursuit of his own identity. They are mistaken who suppose that sex is in itself some way of establishing or proving one's identity or any resolution of the search for selfhood. One who does not know himself and seeks to find himself in sexual experience with another will neither find himself nor respect the person of his sexual partner. Often enough, the very futility of the search for identity in sex will increase the abuse of both one's own self and one's partner. The pursuit of identity in sex ends in destruction, in one form or another, for both the one who seeks himself and the one who is used as the means of the search. No one may show another who he is; no one may give another life; no one can save another.

Where then shall one find who he is as a human being, if sex provides neither the means nor the answer, and thus be emancipated from the power of sin in sex, and in other realms as well?

In Christ.

In Christ. That means in beholding Christ who is in His own person the true man, the man living in the state of reconciliation with God, within himself, with all men, with the whole of creation.

In Christ. That means in discerning that God ends the search for self by Himself coming into this world in search of men. For the man no longer has to find himself who knows that he has been found by God.

In Christ. That means in surrendering to the presence and power of death in all things, including sex, and in that event, in the very midst of death, receiving a new life free from the claim of death.

In Christ. That means in accepting the fact of God's immediate and concretely manifest love for human life, including one's own little life, finding, then, that one's own life is encompassed in God's love for the world.

In Christ. That means in knowing that in the new life which God gives to men there is no more a separation between who a man is and what a man does, but that which he does, in sex or anything else, is the sign of who he is, and that all that he does, become and are sacraments of his new life.

In Christ. That means in realizing radical fulfillment as a person in the life of God in this world, indeed such radical fulfillment that abstinence in sex is a serious option for a Christian though it never be a moral necessity.

In Christ. That means in enjoying God's love for all men and all things in each and every event or decision of one's own life.

In Christ. That means in confessing that all life belongs to God, and but for Him there is no life at all.

4

Work, Witness, and Worship

If the work which any man has built on the foundation survives, he will receive a reward. If any man's work is burned up, he will suffer loss, though he himself will be saved, but only as through fire.

I Corinthians 3:14–15

WORK IS the common means by which men hope and seek to justify their existence.

The legend, in America anyway, is that in either the product or the reward of work a man can find his life morally vindicated. Work is here considered a virtue if it satisfies the conformities of the ethics of success, or if it enriches either in money or possessions or in fame and reputation, or, as a sort of last resort, if it is memorable and remembered in fact by those who survive a man—if it is honored by a man's posterity, even though he be dead and rotting in the grave.

The most false and frivolous part of the legend is, of course, the notion that anyone given good health, the competitive spirit, a tolerance of compromise, a consummate ambition, and a little bit of luck can do anything he sets out to do, or become anyone he wants to become. And, more often than not, a little religion seems to be useful since God is thought to be eager to help those who help themselves.

In America the ethics of success in work give the highest moral significance to taking care of yourself and your wealth first of all and, if possible, never taking care of anyone or anything else. The ethics of success here are an ethics of primitive survival in which the profound moral principle is personal self-interest. Mind you, the expression of that self-interest may not appear in the form of ordinary greed for money and property. It may just as likely take other forms: the lust for power *per se* or for the trappings and condiments of power; or the pursuit of fame or notoriety; or just the quest for a modest security, socially and economically, in which equality is attained because in your stratum of society everybody both has and does the same things. Whatever the case, the ethics invoked are the same: seek first your own material and empirical welfare and you will think you are justified in your existence. Then perhaps you will also think that you are accepted or even admired, or, better still, envied and feared by your fellow man, and that when you are gone, you will be reverenced.

Since there is no escape from death, and since there is also, apparently, no salvation from this awful presence of death, then why not at least build a monument of your reputation or notoriety or wealth or possessions by conforming to these ethics of success? You can at least enjoy what you have while you live and take satisfaction from the prospect that others, whether few or many, will gaze upon your monument when you die, and, with good fortune, even after you die. Make work your monument, make it the reason for your life, and you will survive your death in some way, until the monument itself is discarded or crumbles in some other way.

Work is the common means by which men seek and hope to justify their existence while they are alive and to sustain their existence, in a fashion, after they die.

In the ordinary experience of men, work is intimately associated with the reality of death. But Christians know that work has reference to death in a much more profound way. Christians discern that work is, in itself, a service to death, and that all the myths about success and security, money and social conformity, monuments and posterity do not explain or resolve the activity of death in work. Christians approach the question of the meaning of work and of the relationship of work to the presence and power of death in consideration of and in reliance upon the work of God in the world. Christians see work not in terms of some foolish or fictitious idea of immortality. They see it as a medium in which the power of God over death may be exposed and praised, in which God may be glorified for His triumph over the reign of death. They see the ordinary work men do in the world, from day to day, as a means of witness and, indeed, of worship.

The Meaning of Work

Work is a foretaste—a preliminary experience—of death. That is both the testimony of the Bible and the empirical knowledge of men at work. One has not to look far to observe that for the great multitudes of people throughout the world work is a harsh, relentless burden. Most people in most of the world, not only long ago but today, live in appalling poverty and work not to better themselves or get ahead, but merely in order to maintain their own poverty and indebtedness. This is the case not only for the masses of people in, say, India or Haiti, but also in American society among, for example, migrant workers or the inhabitants of urban slums. Indeed, at the present time, one fourth of all Americans live in poverty.

Yet even among those who are not economically poor, work remains, as a matter of experience, a great burden. Those whose work consists of serving the great corporate principalities, for instance, are subject to dehumanizing, enslaving, frequently idolatrous claims over their lives. Does anyone seriously suppose that the high-ranking executives involved in the price-fixing scandals in some of the great corporations in this country are anything but prisoners, no more truly free than serfs, confined and conformed to the interests of the principalities they serve?

The language of the Bible regarding principalities—the ruling authorities, the angelic powers, the demons, and the like—sounds, I suppose, strange in modern society, but these words in fact refer to familiar realities in contemporary life. The principalities refer to those entities in creation which nowadays are called institutions, ideologies, and images. Thus a nation is a principality. Or the Communist ideology is a principality. Or the public image of a human being, say a movie star or a politician, is a principality. The image or legend of Marilyn Monroe or Franklin Roosevelt is a reality, distinguishable from the person bearing the same name, which survives and has its own existence apart from the existence of the person.

This, too, is the Biblical description of work. In sin men lose their dominion over the creation which God gave them, and their relationship with this creation becomes toil. *"Cursed is the ground because of you; in toil you shall eat of it all the days of your life; thorns and thistles it shall bring forth to you; and you shall eat the plants of the field. In the sweat of your face you shall eat bread till you return to the ground, for out of it you were taken; you are dust, and to dust you shall return." (Gen. 3:17–19)*

Work represents the broken relationship between men and the rest of creation. Men, literally, work to death.

The fallenness of work, the broken relationship between men and the rest of creation which work is, involves both the alienation of men from nature and from the rest of creation, including the principalities and powers. In work men lose their dominion over the principalities and are in bondage to the principalities. Instead of men ruling the great institutions—corporations, unions, and so on— men are ruled by the great institutions. And the claim over a man's life that *all* principalities make is idolatrous, that is, the claim that the significance and destiny of a man depends upon his service to the survival and preservation of the principality. The estrangement between men and the rest of creation means, among other things, the enslavement of men to the institutions for which they work.

Choice of work is largely illusory, too. You cannot choose a job that will save you the burden of death in work. The multitudes of the poor in the world have no choice whatever about the work they will do if, indeed, there is any work for them to do. But even among more economically secure, somewhat educated people the choice of work is largely determined by factors beyond a person's effective control, beyond the scope of a man's freedom. His choice is made or coerced by the ethics of conformity: the preferences, prejudices, and traditions of family, class, or race, the idols of status and success, the lust for money and possessions. And where there is some apparent freedom of choice of a job the essential meaning of work is not changed by the choice.

. . . non-work

Non-work, like work, represents the broken relationship between men and the rest of creation, and, in American society, non-work in its several forms is of increasing significance. Non-work in the sense of unemployment continues to plague American life and embodies not only the threat to life in the obvious terms of economic insecurity and instability, but also, and perhaps more importantly, prolonged, enforced idleness which is profoundly debilitating psychologically. Unemployment caused by mandatory retirement of older persons is particularly depressing since it so often marks the beginning of a period in which an unoccupied person is simply waiting for his own death.

Unemployment, especially in the city, is now joined with the problem of unemployability that results from the accelerating impact of automation on urban life. There are, for example, about a quarter of a million elevator operators in this country, many of whom are middle-aged, most of whom have no other occupational skill, many of whom are Negroes, and almost all of whom face imminent displacement because of the automation of elevators.

Unemployability of vast numbers of people becomes the prospect in many other areas, especially those affecting menial jobs. This is an especially serious problem for young people who have only marginal skills. One statistic shows that by 1970 there will be one unskilled low-paying job for every five youths with less than a high-school education. The ranks of the unemployable of all ages will join those of the retired, the disabled, and the elderly in non-work, in awaiting death.

. . . *leisure*

The most elementary and common form of non-work is, of course, leisure, the time and activities in which men occupy themselves when not at work. Here, too, is evident the broken relationship between men and the rest of creation. The breach that work represents is not healed in leisure, especially in a society like ours where leisure is mainly consumed in highly organized activities designed, it seems, mainly to fill time. The uncritical, if not in fact hypnotic, addiction of many folk to gazing at a television set at every opportunity, day after day and night after night, is but the most crude example. In addition there are those leisure activities pursued in response to commercial indoctrination as to what a person of certain status must have or do to be reassured of his place in society: if you are of one class you must play golf, if another you must bowl, if another drink Scotch, if another join a dance studio, and so on. Leisure has become the commercial exploitation of boredom. It is as much an anticipation of death, as much an enslavement to the world, as work is.

. . . products and rewards

As for the products and rewards of work, they suffer the same end as the worker. They perish, and nothing in or about them has any saving power against the reality of death. It is vain to suppose that either work or non-work, representing, as both do, the alienation of men from the rest of creation, has any efficacy against the power of death's reign. Neither work nor non-work justifies the worker.

There is no sense in which a man can find moral justification in work, despite much talk in the churches to that effect. The burden of work, which is the threat of death, is neither mitigated nor overcome in the choice of work, in the product of work, in the reward for work, in non-work, in the moral vanity of work.

The Work of God for the World

For Christians, work—the analysis of its meaning, the concrete problems of work, the personal experience of work—must be understood in the context of the work of God in the world.

For non-Christians, it may seem an impertinence for Christians to speak of God's work at all.

It is.

It is the very boldness of confession of the Gospel; it is the confession that God has spoken for Himself and that He addresses men in a way that enables them to witness to what He has said and done.

Or it may seem superfluous to non-Christians to speak of the work of God in connection with the work of men. It is enough to deal with one or the other without mixing the two. But this is the very foolishness which announces that the only true work of men is witness to the work of God.

What really scandalizes non-Christians is the confession on the part of Christians that God lives and *works*: that is the awful scandal of the Gospel. To confess God in this way is not an affection for "moral and spiritual values," nor is it a persuasion to some splendid idea of God, or just a religious vocabulary dressing up ordinary social morality, or some sublime speculative truth, but it is confession of God's real presence—His life, power, vitality, action, and working in and for this world.

The critical question, then, about work concerns the identity of Jesus Christ and the work of God in Him for the world. Who is Jesus Christ? What is the work of God in Him for the world?

The work of God in Christ for the world *is the world*. The work of God in Christ is God making the world for Himself. The original and final, the indigenous and present, the fundamental and radical truth about creation is the Lordship of Jesus Christ. Christ is Lord: the world and the work of the world in which men engage belong to Him. Christ is Lord: in Him is the embodiment of human life which is reconciled within itself and at the same time with both God and all things and all men.

The work of God in Christ for the world is *God vindicating Himself in the world*. The hostility of the world to God, the futility of the work of the world in and of itself, the perishing of men in their work, the demands of the principalities—the great institutions and corporations and the like for which men work—none of these threaten or depose Christ as Lord; on the contrary they confirm His Lordship, for in Him God has triumphed over them. In our history, in Christ, God accepts and assumes the fullness of the burden of the rejection of both men and nations. Specifically and climactically in the Crucifixion, He manifests decisively His own identity and power as God and, at the same time, affirms and renews the lives of men in this world.

The work of God in Christ for the world is *God restoring fallen creation to Himself*. In Christ God takes upon Himself the whole burden of the hostility of the world to Him, the futility of work, and even the immediate and ultimate powers of death itself. Thereby are men, in both their lives and work, set free from the threat of death and from the homage death seeks. In Christ there is a new creation. In Christ there is a new birth for men. In Christ God elects the Church, constitutes for Himself a new people who are saved in all things from death. In Christ the world is absolved from the Fall— from the reign of death—and the integrity of creation is rescued and restored.

The work of God in Christ for the world is *God judging the world*. In Christ the mercy of God in reconciling the world to Himself is the event in which the world is judged. Where the Church represents the world reconciled to God and within itself, where the Church lives as Christ's Body, where the Church heralds the judgment of the world by Christ, the Church suffers the same hostility of the world that Christ Himself bore. In that sense, the Church, in the midst of her service to the world and mission in the world, always stands over against the world representing in her own historic life the society that the world is called to be. The Church is thus the exemplification of the work of God for the world.

The work of God in Christ for the world is *God ending the world*. In Christ is God bringing all things and all men to their fulfillment and to their end in Himself. Christ is Lord: as Christ is the beginning, so Christ is the end. The Church lives in constant expectancy of and in readiness for, the consummation of the world in Christ, but the Church lives in this way, not for the sake of herself, but for the sake of the world.

Work as Witness

The work of God in Christ for the world is accomplished in *this* world, in the very world in which men live and work and are dying, in this world which men know from their own ordinary experience. That means that those who witness to God's work in this world are given freedom to confront and cope with the world as it is, without romanticism; without indifference to any actual experience of men at work; without rationalization; without imagining that the world is different from what it is; without evasion; without escape from the real burden of daily work, which is the very burden of death. A mark of the Christian witness is an invariable, unfeigned realism about the world and the work of the world.

For a man to be free in work or in non-work—free from merely working to death, free from enslavement to the principalities and powers—he must be set free from the bondage to death. It is the work of God in Christ for the world that frees men from this bondage and that enables any secular work to become and be a witness to the work of God.

In other words, where Christians take seriously the work of Christ for the world, the question of work is not simply or even essentially ethical. It is *confessional*. The problem is not the moral significance of the daily work of men to God, but, instead, the meaning of the work of God for the common work of men. Work, for the Christian, is not what men do for God's sake, or for their own, but a witness to what God does for the sake of all men and for the sake of the whole world.

All the same, it cannot be overlooked that even Christians, perhaps as often as those who are not Christians, minimize or ignore the work of God when they discuss the work of men in the world. The evidence for this is common enough in Church literature on vocation and work, where there is so much talk of "applying faith to daily work" or of "making the Gospel relevant to secular work." Coming from Christians this is astonishing, for in the Christian faith there is no inherent problem of connecting a god who is some place else—a god of abstract presence and power—with this world. Nor is there any issue of relating a gospel which is about something else—a hypothetical or idealistic gospel—to the life and work of this world. Christ means God in the world. The Gospel of Christ means the work of God in the world for the world. Christ means the creative, comprehensive, specific, and conclusive concern of God for the common life and work of this world.

When Christians do overlook the Word of God, the peril is a disintegration of the Christian life in the world and an immobilization of the Christian mission for the world. Where there is such oversight, the understanding of Christian vocation in daily work becomes, at most, a mere attempt to formulate and articulate some ethics of decision for daily work.

Work as witness is specifically the confession in and through ordinary daily work of the Lordship of Christ, that is, that the whole of creation, despite its fallenness, belongs to God. The fact of Christ's Lordship over the whole of life, including work, means that witness is the only proper work of men, and any employment or occupation may be the instrument of that work.

In Christ is the image of man exercising the dominion over the rest of creation which God first gives to men in creation, and which in sin men lose. And for those who become members of the Body of Christ in the world, dominion is restored. The Christian is a man who, by the work of Christ, has had his own life restored to him, is free from the threat of death in all things, and who lives now in reconciliation with other men and with the rest of creation.

Work as Worship

For such a man daily work, and non-work, become virtually indistinguishable from worship. Worship is not some peculiar cultus practice, some esoteric folk activity, to which Christians resort out of sentiment or superstition, or even for inspiration or self-motivation. On the contrary, worship is the celebration of God's presence and action in the ordinary and everyday life of the world. Worship is not separated or essentially distinguishable from the rest of the Christian life; it is the normative form and expression of the Christian life; it is the integration of the whole of the Christian life into history.

The actions and relationships characteristic of the gathered, sacramental life of the Church in worship are the precedent for the actions and relationships of members of the company of the Church in their involvement in the common life of the world. And, at the same time, the specific involvement of Christians in the life and work of the world every day is the content of that which they offer to God in the corporate worship of the Church. One authenticates the other. And neither can exist with any integrity or much meaning without the other. Worship in the sanctuary is empty unless the Christian in his daily work is engaged in acknowledging and celebrating the work of God for the world. But daily work is not sanctified unless it is offered, encompassed, taken up into the worship of the whole people of the Church in their gathering in the sanctuary.

Remember, too, that in the Christian faith, unlike the practices of some religions, worship does not mean offering to God what it is thought would please or appease Him. In the Gospel men do not sacrifice themselves or their lives or any part of their lives for God. Just the contrary, in the Gospel, God sacrifices His life for men. (That is why, in a sense, there is no such thing as martyrdom in the Christian faith, despite careless talk otherwise.) What Christians offer God in worship, both in the sanctuary and in daily work, is everything—the whole of their lives—all that they have said and done—that which seems good and worthy of themselves as well as that which seems to them evil or unworthy. It is for God's mercy alone to determine what is pleasing to Him. What Christians know, only, is that God cares for the uttermost of a man's life, and claims the whole of a man's life—with nothing reserved, nothing held back, nothing to hide, no matter what.

It is then—when worship is the style and meaning of all that a man is and does—when everything in work or play or talk or deed or thought is included in the offertory—that a man is free from the intimidations of death. Then a man knows and confesses that it is God in whom all life is given and received and made whole.

5

Evangelism, Conversion, Baptism, and Vocation

But in fact Christ has been raised from the dead. . . .
I Corinthians 15:20

So THEN men are always surrounded by witnesses of the presence and vitality of death in this world—in their anxiety and loneliness, in sex and their attempts to find identity and life, in work and the pursuit of success or security or leisure, in fact, in all things. In the face of all that, Christians insist that the fulfillment of life—life which prevails against death and against any and every symptom of death—is in Christ, is the secret of God's work in this world.

But how, then, does one enter into this secret? How does one receive the life constituted in the work of Christ? How does it happen that a man becomes a Christian? What does it mean to be evangelized and converted? And what, in relation to these matters, does it mean to be baptized?

Perhaps no single subject excites such consternation among American Christians as that of the meaning of evangelism as related to conversion and baptism and, then, the practice of the Christian life.

In some regions of the churches, evangelism has become identified and defined in terms of a highly organized, stylized, and stereotyped transaction—in the manner of the so-called mass evangelism of Billy Graham and others. But given the high percentage of active churchpeople that flock to these crusades, one wonders whether what transpires in such events is a form of revivalism only and not evangelism at all.

At the same time evangelism is both unwelcome outside the churches—in the market place, in the forums of secular life—and suppressed within many churches for the same reason, namely, the ready acquiescence of the churches to that peculiar American comity that regards it as a threat to the cohesion and tranquillity of society to confess the Gospel openly or commend the Gospel to another. Evangelism is consigned at most a private and personal status, but it is treated as a matter too vulgar to mention in polite public life. Probably nothing is quite so unpopular in the churches of main-line Protestantism as evangelism.

Meanwhile, most people evidently inherit their affiliation with a church anyway. They are baptized into church membership; they are not, for the most part, brought into the Body of Christ because they have been evangelized and are converted to the Gospel.

The Meaning of Evangelism

Christians are too fond of supposing that evangelism is the work of God. I suggest that it is not.

Evangelism is a work of the Church. Alongside the work of worship and the work of being a servant to the world, evangelism is a characteristic work of the Church. The Church is not mature, indeed, may not be the Church, wherever and whenever the Church is not engaged in all and each of these works.

Remember that none of the disciples who accompanied Jesus during His historic ministry were evangelists. It is only later on, after His earthly ministry, after His crucifixion, after His descent into hell, after His resurrection, after the appearances of the Risen Christ, only at Pentecost that the work of evangelism is commissioned as an essential and characteristic work of the Church. And even then there was dispute about the nature and scope of evangelism, and it is only in the acceptance by Peter and the other apostles of the authority of the evangelist Paul that the work of evangelism is definitely and definitively regarded as a work of the Church in the world.

One suspects that sometimes evangelism is spoken of as the work of God in order to avoid another confusion—that too much attaches to what is called evangelism, that is, the witness of the Church to the Church. Much of the activity and utterance in the churches which is said to be evangelism is in fact not evangelism at all but a mere witness to the Church—or some church—and an invitation to join a church and to support a church and to otherwise serve a church. In any given instance that may or may not be a valid or commendable practice but, whatever it be, it is *not* the work of evangelism.

Evangelism, as a legitimate and necessary task of the Church, is the public proclamation in the world of the presence of the Word of God in the common life of the world, of the presence of the Word of God, in other words, in a way which is accessible to all men for all time.

Evangelism always, therefore, specifically refers to the extraordinary presence of the Word of God in the world in Jesus Christ.

The venerable argument as to whether or not in the tactics of evangelism one finally has to name the Name is answered in the fact that Jesus Christ is the historic, unique, and universal verification of God's presence in this history in this world.

Jesus Christ is the assurance that all of life, the life of every man and of the rest of creation, originates in and ends in the life of God. Your life, or mine, or that of anybody, issues from the Word of God, and this is and remains the essential Truth about you, or me, or anybody, no matter whatever else may be or may seem to be true.

This is of enormous practical significance in the work of evangelism, because it means that evangelism fundamentally is an appeal to a man to remember what is the radical and original Truth of his own birth and being. Evangelism does not bear the Word of God to those to whom the Word is utterly unknown. The evangelist merely calls upon the one whom he addresses to recollect the One who made him and for whom he was made, to recall, as it were, his own creation in the Word of God, to remember who he truly is, to recover his very life.

Thus evangelism is an act of love by the Church, or by a member of the Church, for the world or some person. Evangelism is the act of proclaiming the presence of the Word of God in the life of another, the act of profoundly affirming that person's essential identity and being. And such an affirmation given by one to another *is* love.

Notice that evangelism is a very modest and simple (though not necessarily easy) work. The evangelist is not burdened with bringing the Word of God *de nova* to another, for no man whom the evangelist may address is a stranger to the Word of God by the evidence of his own life, whatever it be, whether he much realizes it or not. Nor is the evangelist particularly concerned with apologetics, with defending or explaining or arguing about the Gospel. Nor is the evangelist engaged much in trying to persuade another that the Gospel is true or relevant or objective or whatnot; rather, the evangelist is engaged in loving the other in a way that calls upon the other to accept himself in the same way. The evangelist is engaged in exposing to another who he is and exposing to him, whoever he is, that he is loved by God and thus set free to be who he is.

Evangelism and Conversion

Evangelism is a work of the Church; conversion is a work of God. Evangelism calls upon men to remember and recognize the presence and activity of God in their own particular lives. Conversion is the event of that recall and recognition.

Put aside the unfortunate connotations that have become associated with the word *conversion*. Conversion means, simply, the event of becoming a Christian. Put aside, too, stereotyped notions as to the pattern, sequence, accompanying signs of conversion. (Or, to put it a bit differently, the fact that Paul is commonly depicted, in the course of the event of his conversion, as having been struck off his horse does not mean that it is characteristic of other conversions that one falls off a horse.) Consider conversion first of all as the response to evangelism, as the reality of remembrance of identity which the evangelist in his work has first of all affirmed.

The event of becoming a Christian is the event in which a man utterly and unequivocally confronts the presence and power of death in and over his own existence, and, in the same event, is exposed to the presence and power of God overwhelming death in his own existence.

Conversion is the personal experience, within the course of one's present life, of one's own death and of one's own resurrection.

It is *really* death that is here involved.

In conversion a man suffers the complete recall of his own biography and history. All that he is and has been, all that he has done, everything that he has said, all whom he has met, every place

53

where he has been, every fragment and facet of his experience and existence—*everything* is subject to his own consciousness that he has been and is consigned to death, serving death, bonded to death, in fact dying. Conversion is the event in which a man finds himself radically and absolutely helpless. The event of becoming a Christian is a man seeing that he is, in every respect, naked, exposed, transparent—completely vulnerable. Conversion means the overpowering reality of a man's *own* death against which he is without capability of resistance in any fashion whatever. Conversion is such an intimacy with the presence and reality of death in the world, and in and within one's own life in the world, that on the day of the undertaker, when a man is carted away and submitted to the earth and, with any sort of luck, honored by an obituary, on that day the one who is converted will know nothing, will suffer nothing which he has not already known and suffered in his conversion, in his death in Christ.

But as, in conversion, a man already suffers his own death, so, also, in the same event, does he receive the freedom from the power of death which is the resurrection. Conversion is an ultimate and radically personal exposure to death, but in the same event, it is the ultimate and immediately personal exposure to the power of God overcoming death. Conversion is death *in Christ.*

Conversion does not, characteristically, happen in a moment. It is, of course, not at all beyond God's grace to work the conversion of a man in a single moment, but there are virtually no authenticated reports of literally momentary conversions in the New Testament or in the history of the Church. Moreover, conversion is in itself an event that transcends the ordinary and familiar dimensions of time, for the event itself encompasses the whole recall of a man's biography and anticipates as well the end and fulfillment of a man's life eschatologically. Attempts to fix a specific moment as *the* moment of conversion fail to take seriously that conversion is the work of God in a particular man's life, not a work of the Church, not a work of an evangelist, and not something sought or attained in any sense by the one converted. Rather, indeed, than speak of conversion within a moment of time, it is more fitting to speak of conversion as an event that shatters the categories of time and emancipates a man from bondage to time, which is, after all, a sign of bondage to death.

That momentary conversion, if it ever happens, is rare is clear from the reports of that conversion about which there is more information than perhaps any other conversion in the whole history of the Christian people—the conversion of Paul. Paul had no modesty about his conversion; he boasted of it every time he uttered or wrote a word. (He is, thus, a good example for Christians nowadays.)

Paul's conversion was not a brief or momentary event. On the contrary, he was struck down, felled from his horse, blinded, remained in blindness for some days, then entered and stayed in the wilderness for a long time—one account reports that it was ten years. Only thereafter did Paul emerge and begin to practice his vocation and ministry as a Christian.

Notice some other things about Paul's conversion, apart from the matter of time. For one thing, Paul's conversion was a thoroughly traumatic event—his whole being suffered the impact. He was not only physically afflicted, but he apparently was incapacitated—immobilized—so far as the usual human activities are concerned for as long as he remained in the wilderness. The wilderness experience, I suggest, is integral to the conversion. It is not at all a time of contemplation—in the sense of the Oriental ascetics. Specifically, to be in the wilderness represents the concrete encounter with death. To be in the wilderness is to be present with the singular reality of one's own death and to be confronted with the reign of death in all the world. But the wilderness is also a place into which Christ Himself has come and in which Christ has already been victorious over the claims and temptations of death. Paul entered the wilderness in his conversion and beheld the triumph of Christ in the wilderness; Paul went into the wilderness and was there protected from death by Christ.

The work of God which is conversion is truly saving in the most personal sense. There is not—as some folk vainly preach—an element of self-denial or restriction in conversion. The converted man does not denounce or give up what he was before as a person, but what he was before as a person is, in conversion, restored to him in maturity and fulfillment. It was so with Paul—who was a great zealot. Before his conversion, Paul was the most zealous persecutor of Christ. After his conversion, Paul becomes the most zealous evangelist and apologist. Both before and after, Paul is still Paul the zealot. Paul is still the person he is in every sense, save that now that which he is, is freed from tribute to death and fulfilled—made new—brought to mature humanity—in Christ.

So the work of God which is conversion is a work that frees a man to be the man whom the evangelist has recognized and affirms.

Conversion, Baptism, and Vocation

A man who is converted will be baptized; that is, in the midst of the Church he will confess the faith, and his confession will be confirmed by the Church and the members of the Church, and he will be welcomed into the company of the Church. But what of the practice of baptism where the one baptized has not yet been converted and does not confess the faith, as is the case in infant baptism?

In the first instance such baptism is not an act of the child baptized, but an act of the Church on behalf of the child, an act in which the Church, and the people of the Church both individually and corporately, confess that they trust the Gospel so much that they believe that the power of God will save this child from death. The Church confesses that the grace of God which has been sufficient to save the members of the Church is also sufficient for this child. And the Church and the members of the Church then commit themselves to raise and nurture, to love, this person in such a way that he will come to a full maturity in Christ and himself confess the faith.

Too often baptism is profaned in the churches, and, it seems, churchpeople do not realize what a radical action and responsibility is involved in baptizing a child. But even though that be the case, the grace of God is not vitiated by the stupidity or frivolity of Christians. Even though Christians sometimes invoke the name of God but do not take the matter seriously, God does. The name of God may be invoked vainly, but that Name is never invoked in vain. The sufficiency of God's mercy is enough for the child even where the Church falters in her responsibility for the child, even when the people of the Church fail to love the child and his maturing in Christ.

To often, also, baptism is misunderstood profoundly. It is widely thought to be the sacrament of the unity of the Church, but that is not what baptism is, much less being a mere membership or initiation ritual. Baptism is the assurance—accepted, enacted, verified, and represented by Christians—of the unity of *all men* in Christ. The baptized are the people in history consecrated to the unity men receive in the worship of God. The oneness of the Church is the example and guarantee of the reconciliation of all men to God, and of the unity of all men and all creation in the life of God. The Church, the baptized society, is called to be the image of all mankind, the one and intimate community of God.

Baptism is the sacrament of the extraordinary unity among men wrought by God in overcoming the power and reign of death, in overcoming, that is, all that alienates, segregates, divides, and destroys men in their relations to each other, indeed also within their own persons, and in their relationship with the rest of creation.

Thus the vocation of the baptized person is a simple thing: it is to live from day to day, whatever the day brings, in this extraordinary unity, in this reconciliation with all men and all things, in this knowledge that death has no more power, in this truth of the Resurrection. It does not really matter what exactly a Christian does from day to day. What matters is that in whatever he does it is done in honor of the triumph of Christ over death and, therefore, in honor of his own life, given to him by God and restored to him in Christ, and in honor of the life into which all men and all things are called. The only thing that really matters is to live in Christ instead of death.

Suggestions for Group Study

Prepared by the Youth Division
Department of Christian Education
Protestant Episcopal Church

THIS IS a book about some very common issues of life: loneliness, sex and the search for identity, the meaning of work—and the death that is common to them all. It is, in addition, a book about life in Christ, and the place and meaning of conversion.

Even though the issues dealt with are common ones, they are not commonly understood at the depth the author treats them. The book is therefore not an easy one, but it fully merits careful study and will fully reward those who undertake it.

Recommended Age-Groups

This book can be used in a group comprising tenth-, eleventh-, and twelfth-graders. In its entirety it will probably be a bit steep for tenth-graders alone, though parts of it can certainly be used. Adults and those of college age can also use it satisfactorily. This guide, however, is prepared for use with older senior highs.

Basic Requirement

Each participant must have a copy of the text.

Leadership

The first key to the successful study of *Instead of Death* lies in the adult leader's ability to share in the learning experience at some depth with the group members. Because the issues dealt with strike at the root of the existence of all of us, regardless of age, a high degree of rapport and mutual respect must exist within the group for anyone to be able to respond freely to what the author is saying.

Structure

What has become known as the "small group plan" of youth work is the most desirable format for a study of this depth. Since that plan involves a closed group, whose members are committed to attendance, trust can be established; it is an excellent size (8–10) for free discussion; it has a life of approximately three months (none too long for a thorough study of *Instead of Death*).

If, however, you are not working within this kind of structure, try to work in groups as small as possible. A group of thirty or forty persons might meet in one large room, but at tables seating only eight. Keep the table groups as constant as possible throughout the study. Certain "warm-up" questions can be considered by the group as a whole, but the reading and discussion questions can best be handled by the table groups. Young people can take turns serving as leaders of these table groups, following the suggestions for each chapter as outlined in this guide.

Where the suggestion in the guide calls for reading aloud, let participants take turns reading a paragraph or a page at a time. Others should follow the reading in their own copies, unless other directions are given.

To Do Ahead of Time

The adult leader or leaders should read and reread the text. It is essential to get the full sweep of what the author is saying so that all the parts are seen within the whole, not out of context.

In addition to a copy of the text for each participant, paper and pencils should be kept on hand for everyone. Newsprint and marker or a blackboard are also essential tools.

In relation to Chapter 3, the leader would do well to familiarize himself with Evelyn M. Duval's *Love and the Facts of Life* (Association, 1963). It is a revision of the old favorite *Facts of Life and Love for Teen-Agers,* and presents a more realistic picture of today's young people than the earlier volume.

Leading Young People (Seabury) and *You Can't Be Human Alone* (Seabury and others) are good basic guides for those who wish more help in organizing and leading effective discussion groups.

Number of Sessions Required
(Three alternative plans)

(Each session approximately 1½ hours)

(Pick up Chapter 4 at some other time in the year.)

CHAPTER 1

Before beginning to read, ask the group this question: "When you think of death, what do you think of?" (Hand out paper and pencil and let the members think and write. Let them share briefly with each other what they have written. Then hand out the book— and let the title, *"Instead* of Death," begin to sink in.)

1. Read out loud, starting with the Biblical quotation and ending at the first subheading.
   a. Do you agree with the author that the common issues of life are the same for *all* people, regardless of where they live? Why or why not?

b. The author has listed the common issues with which he proposes to deal as: loneliness, sex and the search for personal identity, work, leisure, and security. How does he say these issues are related to each other?

c. What does the author say we all have in common with one another?

d. Ann-Marie's cousin Alan has just been in a terrible automobile accident and is in the hospital with a fractured skull. Ann-Marie's mother is sure this happened to Alan because he lied to his father last week about how much money he paid for his new guitar. "God did this to punish him," Ann-Marie's mother said to her. In reporting this to her church youth group, Ann-Marie says, "I don't know whether to believe her or not." How would you reply?

2. Now read aloud the section called *Death, Evil, and Sin.* Discuss, with the help of these questions:

a. Would you now answer Ann-Marie's question any differently? How?

b. According to the author, Ann-Marie's mother, in claiming that the automobile accident was God's way of punishing Alan, was in effect saying that she knows how God judges. Do you agree that this is a way of "playing God"?

c. What does the author call this tendency to "play God"?

d. What happens when people do this? What happens when you do it?

3. Now read the section called *Death and Youth.*
   Do you agree that even young people are involved with the issues of death? Why or why not?

4. Read aloud to the end of the chapter.

a. Why is it, do you think, that people do not often talk frankly about death and yet like to watch auto stunt drivers or other forms of dangerous sport, to say nothing of participating in them themselves? (Do *you* enjoy watching horror films on T.V.? Why or why not?)

b. What more than biological extinction does the author say death is?

c. What does the author say is the last word? (Spend the time between now and the next session thinking over to what degree you really agree with him.)

CHAPTER 2

1. Read aloud the section ending at the first subhead. Discuss, with the aid of these questions:
   a. Do you think there is anyone who has not experienced loneliness?
   b. Do you think young people feel lonely some of the time? Most of the time?
   c. When do *you* feel most lonely? Can you say why you feel lonely at those times?
   d. What do you do to overcome this loneliness?
(Have someone record the answers to d on newsprint.)

2. Now read the section headed *Fictions of Loneliness.*
   a. Were any of your answers to 1d included among the fictions mentioned by the author? Which ones?
   b. What activities does the author mention that you did not?
   c. Do you agree that these "escapes" from loneliness never really overcome loneliness? Why or why not?
   d. Had it ever occurred to you before that in seeking to overcome your loneliness you are really seeking to discover who you are? Do you think this is a valid understanding?

3. Have two good readers read the next section, *Loneliness as a Foretaste of Death,* aloud to the group, alternating paragraphs. The others in the group need not follow the reading in their own books unless they wish to. They should be encouraged to listen to what is being read as they would listen to a meditation. This is an excellent meditation for self-examination. There are no questions to discuss on this section, but after the reading let the group respond in any way they like. They may want to open their own copies and read the passage to themselves, silently.

4. Read aloud the section *The Surrender to Death and the Triumph of Grace* down to the break in the text.
   Can you think of any additional illustrations of the "lonely Christ"?

5. Read aloud to the end of the section. Spend some time quietly thinking about what it says, and about this question: Can you believe it is death that is alone, not you?

6. Again ask two good readers to read the last section, *Loneliness and the Ethics of Holiness*, aloud, alternating paragraphs.
   a. Let group members react to what they heard if they wish to react.
   b. Ask the group to turn to the beginning of the chapter and reread the Biblical quotation. Explain that it is St. Paul speaking, describing an affliction of his and how he had begged the Lord three times to remove the affliction from him. Give group members paper and pencil and ask them, in the light of the chapter they have just read, to write down in their own words what they think the Lord's reply to St. Paul means. After about ten minutes for thinking and writing, let the members share with each other what they have written.

CHAPTER 3

1. Read aloud down to the first subhead.
   a. What does the author say is the most prevalent aspect of sex? What else does he say about this "most prevalent aspect"?
   b. What does the author say is the essential content of what the Gospel has to say about sex?
   c. Do you agree that it is not only all right but appropriate to speak of sex within the church? Why or why not?

2. Let group members read the next section, *Sex and the Sanctuary*, to themselves. Give them pencil and paper and let each person write down topics under this heading: "Aspects of sex that I wish *we* could talk about here." Explain that you are not interested in who writes what, but in the total list representing their thinking. Collect the papers after about five minutes, being careful at this point not to look at their contents. Keep the papers and check off any questions that are answered during the discussion of this chapter. Make definite plans to see that the rest are answered at a specific time in the future if they cannot be handled right away. (For a course on the Theological Understanding of Sex, write to the Youth Division, 815 Second Avenue, New York 17, New

York.) Close the study of this section by a brief discussion of the following:
Can you think of any relationship between persons that does not have some sexual aspect?

3. Read the next section, *The Notion of Christian Marriage*, aloud.
   a. What ideas are new to you in this section? Discuss them.
   b. What does the author mean when he says that marriage is a "fallen estate"? (You may wish to look at St. Matthew 22:23–30 at the conclusion of your discussion of this question.)
   c. What does the author say is the same about a marriage between Christians and a marriage between non-Christians? What does he say is unique about marriage between Christians?

4. Let the group read the section *Sex and Society* silently.
   a. What does the author say about the relationship between sin and the judgments of society? Do you agree? Why or why not?
   b. What does society label as criminally or otherwise antisocial?
   c. Do you agree that if the act committed has no antisocial aspects, the privacy of the individuals involved should be respected? Why or why not?
   d. Does this mean that any such act is not harmful in other ways to the persons involved, or does it mean that it is none of society's business whether or not it is harmful to them in other ways?

Discussion of the next section, *Sex and Adolescence* (questions 5 through 7), may be entered into more freely if the group is divided in two, all boys in one group, girls in the other. However, this may not always be the case. Make your own decision on the basis of the maturity of your group members and the degree of trust they have in you and in one another. If you decide to divide the group, bring them together after a certain time and let a panel made up of two members from each group report what they have chosen to report, or ask of the opposite sex any questions they wish to ask. (If the group is not divided, skip the references to the panel made below.)

5. Read aloud as far as the subhead *Cosmetics and Clothing.*
   a. What would you say are the prevailing sexual mores among young people in *your* community?
   b. How would you rank the perils enumerated by the author? Can you name others?
   c. How effective are these perils in deterring sexual promiscuity in your community?
   d. What reasons can you give besides perils for not indulging in sexual promiscuity? What reasons are generally given for indulging in it?

   (At this point you may wish to refer to the song "Love in Bloom" if you have a copy of the published script of the musical revue *For Heaven's Sake.* The script is available from Baker's Plays, 100 Summer Street, Boston 10, Massachusetts, for $1.50, price subject to change.)

   e. What part does conformity play in your answers to d?
   f. How can you be a conformist and still be a person in your own right, or can't you?

6. Read the section *Cosmetics and Clothes* silently.
   a. Each year some young persons go to overseas countries in the International Christian Youth Exchange or similar programs. In countries where girls do not use cosmetics, American girls tend to abandon them too. Yet even those who seem to like this custom resume use of cosmetics after they return to the United States. What would *you* do in similar circumstances? What does this say about the power of conformity?
   b. Do you agree there are signs that people in America, including young people, are losing a sense of what it means to be masculine and feminine? Give some illustrations in defense of your answer.

7. Read the sections *Pornography, Masturbation,* and *Homosexuality* silently.
   a. How much pornography is available in your community? How do you know?

b. Why do *you* think it has the appeal it does?

c. What can be done to eliminate pornography?

d. What helps does the Church offer to those who have been hurt by harmful sex practices?

e. What further questions do you have on these topics?

8. If the group has been divided for the discussion of questions 5 through 7, let each subgroup now decide what part or parts of this discussion they would like to share with the boys (girls). What questions about any of these topics would they like to address to the boys (girls)? Ask each group to choose two representatives to speak for them.

Hold the panel discussion. Let the four panelists question one another after each has reported. Questions can also be addressed to and from the floor.

9. Read aloud the section *Sex and Sin.*

a. What is added in this treatment of sin to that already given in Chapter 1, page 10? What is the same?

b. What does the author say is sinful in sexual behavior?

c. If people really believed this, what effect do you think it would have, for example, on adolescent sexual practices?

10. Ask two people to read the last section, *Sex and the Search for Self,* aloud, the second reader beginning with the first "In Christ" and alternating paragraphs thereafter.

Hand out paper and pencil and let each person write in his own words what this last section has communicated to him about his own search for identity. Let each share what he has written.

CHAPTER 4

1. Before beginning to read this chapter, ask group members what they think it means when a person is known to be successful in his work. In other words, what does success in a job mean to people today? Record the answers briefly on a blackboard or newsprint.

2. Let the group read silently to themselves down to the first subhead. Explain that the author has packed into these first para-

graphs something of a synopsis of what is to come later, and they should not worry if they do not understand all of it at this point.

    a. What agreement and/or disagreement do you find in the text with your own ideas of an "ethics of success"?

    b. Do you think it is reasonable to try to justify your existence by the quality of the work you do? Why or why not?

3. Read aloud the section headed *The Meaning of Work* down to the subhead *Non-work.*

    a. Do you think work is a burden for most people?

    b. What makes it such, or possibly keeps it from being such?

    c. Why does the author speak of today's big corporations as "principalities"? (Do you know what the "price-fixing scandals" were?) Look at Ephesians 6:10–12.

    d. Why does the author define work as a sign of the broken relationship between man and the rest of creation?

    e. Name some of the elements that limit *your* choice of work right now. Which ones do you expect to encounter in the future?

4. Let everyone read silently down to *The Work of God for the World.*

    a. Do you think that leisure is really as much of an anticipation of death as unemployment is?

    b. Why do you suppose labor unions and others are continually campaigning for shorter work hours? What will this mean for the individuals involved?

5. Read, again silently, the section *The Work of God for the World.* The author singles out certain mighty acts of God for the world: the creation of the world itself; the crucifixion of Christ; the resurrection of Christ; the Lordship of Christ; the new creation in Christ; the judgment of the world by Christ; the fulfillment of the world in Christ. What evidence can you cite for the continuing work of Christ in the world? Look, for example, at the great issues of war and peace; of race; of justice in and through the courts. What others can you think of?

6. Read aloud the last two sections, *Work as Witness* and *Work as Worship*.
   a. Where does the author indicate that the meaning of work is found for a Christian?
   b. What does this mean for you *right now?*
   c. What does the Christian offer to God in worship?
   d. What does this mean for you *right now?*
   e. If a Christian in his daily work is witnessing to, pointing to, what *God* has done and is doing in His world, and if the same Christian in his worship is offering to God *his* daily involvement in the world, then why do you think so many Christians have difficulty seeing the relationship between their daily lives and their Sunday worship?

CHAPTER 5

1. Read down to the first subhead silently.
   a. How did *you* come into church membership?
   b. If it was by conviction, how did you come to get that conviction?
   c. Do you think the Gospel *should* be openly confessed and commended to one another? If so, under what circumstances? By whom? Why?

2. Read silently the section *The Meaning of Evangelism* and discuss 1c (above) again.

3. Read aloud "Chris's Story" (below), taken from the 1963–64 edition of the E.Y.C. Notebook for which Chris wrote it. At the end, try to answer the question that follows.

Chris's Story

MY WRITING this story for you reminds me of a movie I have seen in which was depicted the struggles of an alcoholic. After hospitalization during which he was "dried out" he attended his first meeting with a local group of Alcoholics Anonymous. What a victory it was for this man to stand before a group of strangers and say, "My name is _____, I'm an alcoholic!" This was not to say that he had been cured but that he had found a way in which he could live with his illness.

As I write, a Lenten Season is coming to a close and Easter is only a couple of weeks away. I am once again reminded that the victory of the Galilean gives me the power, the joy, and the compulsion to proclaim, "My name is Chris, I'm a Christian!" But there is something that I had to be able to say first, and I shall go on with my story.

I want to tell you about an incident in my life. I would prefer to say that I want to share it with you, not as a "true confession" or something to be put into one of those newspaper columns of syndicated psychology, but only as an incident with some issues with which I hope you can identify.

I was born and brought up in a suburb of one of our larger cities. I don't come from a broken home, my parents are not, nor were they ever, drunks or fighters. As far as I am concerned, they were never either too strict or too lenient.

Perhaps most of you have heard of the more raw forms of juvenile delinquency. I hope that you have heard more about them than you have ever seen or encountered. The incident which I am about to depict comes out of my experience in this way of life. Of course, I must change some names.

I was a member of the Knights, a group of about fifteen teenagers who were allied with the Satan's Angels. The Satan's Angels were a much larger group than ours, and their membership ranged in age from fifteen to twenty-five. The usual implements of "war" could be found in our midst: pipes, wrapped tire chains, blades, garrison belts with sharpened buckles, etc. And the usual uniform was to be seen: studded leather jackets, engineers' boots, "D.A.'s" and sideburns.

Purpose and meaning? A good question to which we thought we had good answers. We lived in an area that was studded with such legions of honor. To put it in words that I would not have chosen years ago, we wanted defense, security, fellowship, and a feeling of belonging to something strong, tough, and demanding. We had "territory" to defend and "competition" to eliminate. A summer recreation area in our town made our territory most vulnerable to invasion, especially on summer nights. This way of life, I was convinced, gave me what I wanted, including purpose and meaning.

In the mid-afternoon of one July the third, I was found by eight or ten "rivals" on the main street of my home town. They asked me no questions but surrounded me in a circle and began slashing with their belts. When they decided I'd had enough, they got into their car. I began walking; I'd sooner be damned than run like a scared chicken. They drove close to me for almost a tenth of a mile, delighting themselves with competing to see which one of them could spit on me the most.

Was I humbled, scared, able to forgive? No. I resolved that the Knights and the Satan's Angels would revenge. Two days later, I met a close friend who prided himself on being the youngest member of the Satan's Angels. It was quite obvious that he too had been beaten.

"Who did it?"

"The Rebels, from _____."

I knew the Rebels. I'll never forget the first time I had seen them in action. They had busted up a dance in a neighboring town and had followed some of the kids from the dance to a restaurant where some of us had gathered after a high-school basketball game. One of them had pulled a knife on the captain of our team. Another had belted a guy against the roof of his car while his date watched in terror.

"How many of them were there? What kind of car were they driving?" I asked my friend.

"About ten. They were in an old, grey Dodge."

Satan's Angel's had already planned their revenge and avenge for their youngest member's beating. They agreed to double their efforts for my sake. The Rebels' hangout was a movie theater. The Satan's Angels picked up two guys in front of the theater the next night, drove them a few miles, and beat them unmercifully, one for my friend and one for me. The wider the circle of revenge got, the worse the beatings became. Sometimes an all-out rumble was the only way to settle things. This particular circle was not to be closed for a long time.

A short time later, and almost at the same time, two more beatings took place; one of them was in the territory of the Satan's Angels, and the other was in my own territory.

Paul wasn't a member of the Satan's Angels, but I had worked in a country club in their town where he had been head caddy. They made him head caddy because he had had polio and couldn't walk very well. We were close friends. He had given me a lot of good breaks on the job.

Paul was attacked at a pizza joint by two guys who were twice his size. That was in '57 when Ford had produced a car with sharp tail fins. When they had finished beating Paul, they threw him against the tail fins, face first. Paul is now blind in one eye.

The second beating was closer to home than I had bargained for. I was in bed when the police carried my brother into the house. He and two friends had been approached by a group of over twenty while they were innocently having a late-night snack at a roadside eating place.

"Do you guys know anyone who owns a black convertible?" was the only question asked. Well, how many of you know anyone who owns a black convertible? They were torn from their car, beaten and kicked. The car had been smashed with lead pipes. The circle of revenge had gotten wider, the beatings worse, although I had no idea whether or not Paul's and my brother's beatings were related to the ones for which I was responsible.

But here were two innocent people, among others, one of my own flesh and blood, paying for my irrational behavior in what I suddenly realized was an irrational way of life. Paul certainly had not "asked" for what he got. And my brother had never been involved in this kind of life. He didn't know how to defend himself and had never cared. He and I led two very different lives and were, as many brothers are, avowed enemies.

Physical beating by a gang is nothing as compared to the mental torture involved. What we had thought was justice had resulted in the terrible misuse and hurting of persons.

There was no vision of God, no overwhelming emotional experience that swept me into green pastures and beside still waters. I found only myself saying, "My name is Chris, I am rotten, lifeless, sick, lonely, blind, and crippled."

Chris concludes his story with the confession that made it possible for him to say, at the beginning, "I am a Christian." Why was his confession of depravity essential to the beginning of his new life in Christ?

4. Read silently the section *Evangelism and Conversion.*
   a. What have you learned that helps you understand "Chris's Story" better?
   b. In what ways can you now see that Chris had encountered the reign of death in the world—and in his own life?

5. Read out loud the final section, *Conversion, Baptism, and Vocation?*
   a. Have you learned anything new in this section? What?
   b. How does the author define baptism?
   c. Why, then, is the *dis*unity of the Church so tragic?

INSTEAD OF DEATH

BY WILLIAM STRINGFELLOW

Loneliness, sex and the search for identity, the meaning of work—these are some of our common concerns today; and there is a factor common to all of them—death! This book is written to help everyone, and particularly young people, come to grips with these issues and understand them in depth. But it does not stop there; it is a book about resurrection as well as death. It is a book about life in Christ, the only life through which we can know our true identity and find our true vocation in the midst of our complex, twentieth-century culture. A leader's guide, included in the book, makes this study ideal for group use with both young people and adults.

WILLIAM STRINGFELLOW, practicing attorney and partner in a New York law firm, is among the most active Protestant laymen of this decade. He is known in this country and abroad for his active participation in the ecumenical movement and in youth and college work. A popular lecturer, he has spoken at colleges and seminaries in all parts of the country. In addition to articles in law and theological journals, he has written two full-length books, *A Private and Public Faith* and the Seabury Lenten Book for 1964.

THE SEABURY PRESS • NEW YORK